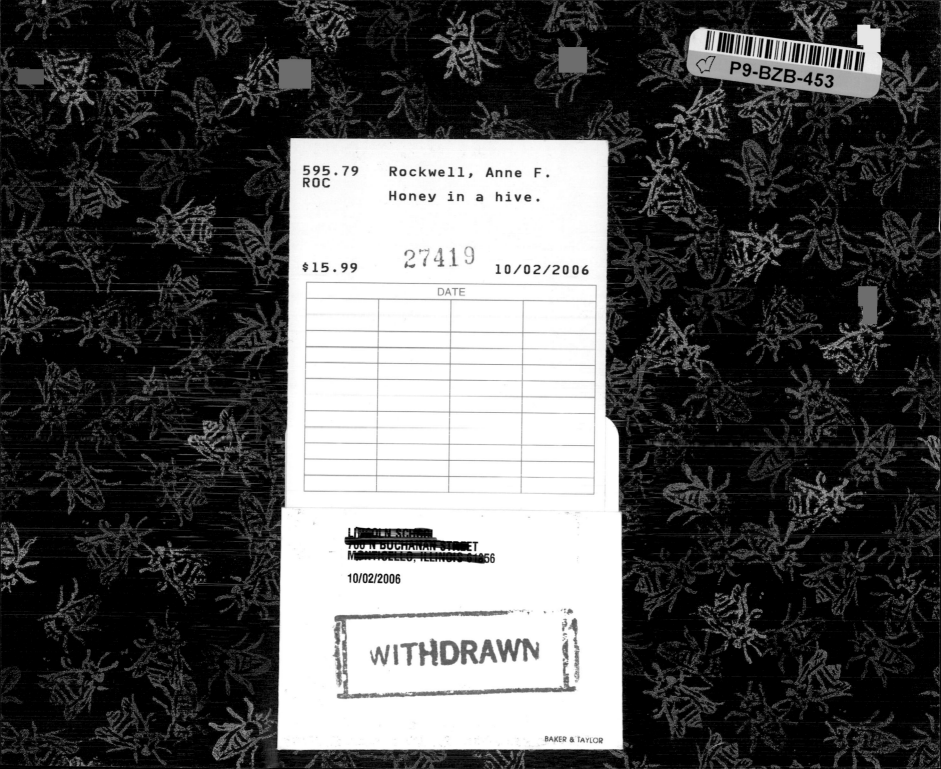

P9-BZB-453

STAGE 2

Honey in a Hive

by Anne Rockwell • illustrated by S. D. Schindler

HarperCollinsPublishers

The *Let's-Read-and-Find-Out Science* book series was originated by Dr. Franklyn M. Branley, Astronomer Emeritus and former Chairman of the American Museum–Hayden Planetarium, and was formerly co-edited by him and Dr. Roma Gans, Professor Emeritus of Childhood Education, Teachers College, Columbia University. Text and illustrations for each of the books in the series are checked for accuracy by an expert in the relevant field. For more information about Let's-Read-and-Find-Out Science books, write to HarperCollins Children's Books, 1350 Avenue of the Americas, New York, NY 10019, or visit our website at www.letsreadandfindout.com.

HarperCollins®, ◢◣®, and Let's Read-and-Find-Out Science® are trademarks of HarperCollins Publishers Inc.

Library of Congress Cataloging-in-Publication Data
Rockwell, Anne F.
  Honey in a hive / by Anne Rockwell ; illustrated by S. D. Schindler.
    p.   cm. — (Let's-read-and-find-out science. Stage 2)
  Summary: An introduction to the behavior and life cycle of honeybees, with particular emphasis on the production of honey.
  ISBN 0-06-028566-4 — ISBN 0-06-028567-2 (lib. bdg.) — ISBN 0-06-445204-2 (pbk.)
  1. Honeybee—Juvenile literature. 2. Beehives—Juvenile literature. 3. Honey—Juvenile literature. [1. Honeybee.
2. Bees. 3. Beehives. 4. Honey.] I. Schindler, S. D., ill. II. Title. III. Series.
  QL568.A6R58 2005   2003010357
  595.79'9—dc21

Typography by Elynn Cohen   2 3 4 5 6 7 8 9 10 ❖   First Edition

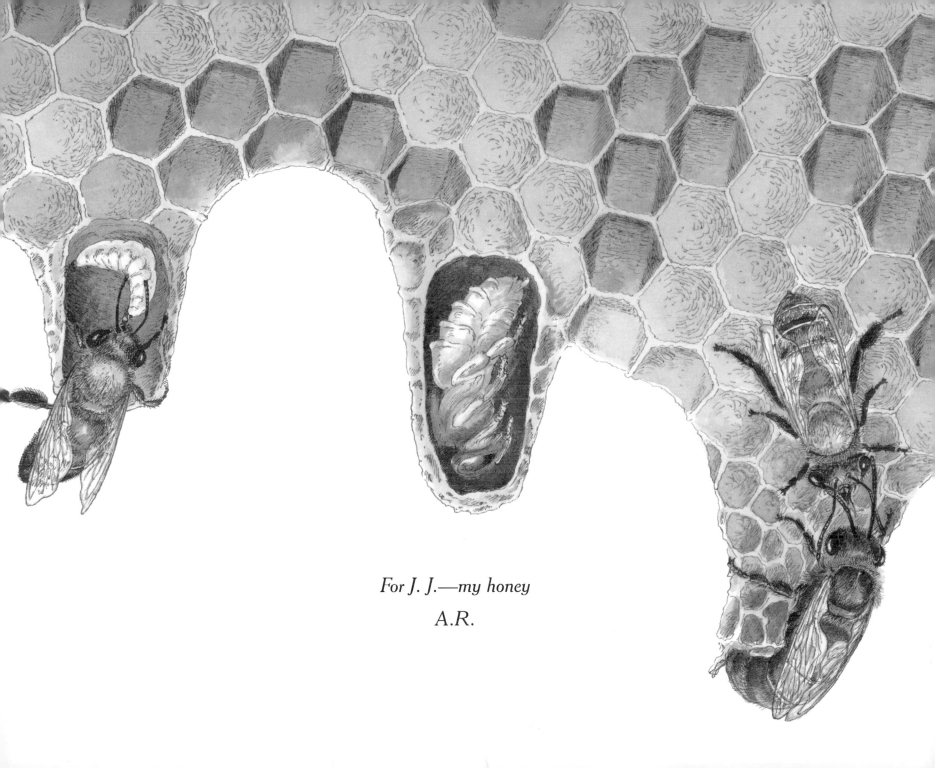

For J. J.—my honey
A.R.

In spring and summer, this meadow is full of sweet-smelling flowers. Listen! Do you hear a buzzing sound? It comes from the rapidly beating wings of many busy bees.

5

They are busy gathering nectar, the sweet liquid inside flowers, to make into honey. They are gathering pollen, the yellow powder in a flower, to feed their queen and all her young bees.

6

Bees live in hives filled with honeycombs that they build with beeswax from their bodies. In every beehive there are thousands of bees and one queen, who is much bigger than any of the other bees. She doesn't gather nectar or pollen or do any work. Her job is to lay eggs that will become new bees.

The queen bee leaves her home to fly high in the sky and mate with many male bees, called drones. Drones don't do any work, either. All they do is mate with the queen so she can lay thousands of eggs. As soon as they have mated with her, they die.

Most bees that hatch inside a hive are worker bees, because there is a lot of work to be done making honey. And workers do all the work—not the drones, not the queen.

All workers are female, but they don't mate or lay eggs.
They gather food, guard and clean the hive, make honey,
and feed their queen and her newly hatched bees. The
food bees eat is honey made from nectar.

13

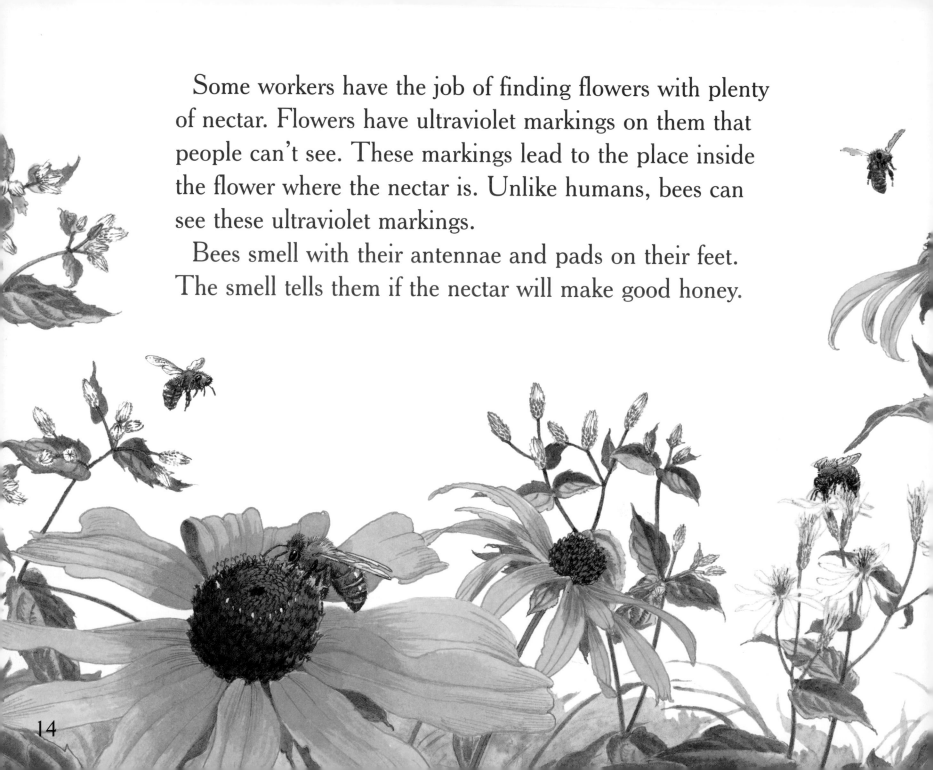

Some workers have the job of finding flowers with plenty of nectar. Flowers have ultraviolet markings on them that people can't see. These markings lead to the place inside the flower where the nectar is. Unlike humans, bees can see these ultraviolet markings.

Bees smell with their antennae and pads on their feet. The smell tells them if the nectar will make good honey.

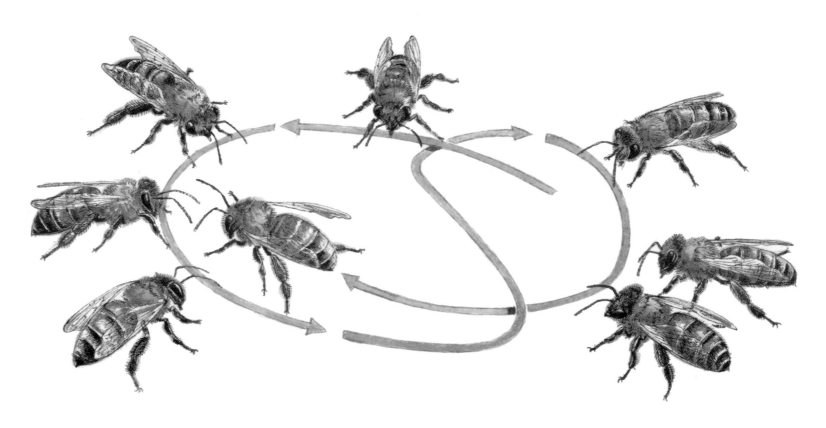

When a worker finds a field full of flowers, she needs help
in gathering nectar from it. She flies back to the hive and does
a dance. The dance tells other worker bees where the flowers
are. As soon as the worker has finished dancing, other worker
bees fly out of the hive and follow her to the flowers.

It takes a lot of nectar to make a little bit of honey. The bees
can't carry much nectar or pollen. They must make many
journeys from the hive to the flowers and back again.

After a worker bee has made about 400 long flights, the muscles in her wings and legs are worn out. She usually falls to the ground and dies of exhaustion.

When a worker brings nectar to the hive, she puts it in a hexagonal, or six-sided, chamber made out of thin wax. These chambers are called cells. Then she flies off to get some more nectar, while other workers get busy turning the nectar into honey.

17

Bees fan the nectar with their wings. This dries the watery nectar so that it becomes thick and sticky. It becomes honey.

Honey's thickness and natural plant chemicals keep germs from growing in the honey. It can be stored in the honeycomb chambers for a long time, sometimes for years.

When a wax chamber is full of honey, the workers seal it up and begin to make a new one. Each cell is exactly the same size and same shape as the others.

More nectar is brought, and more honey is made. More thin-walled wax cells are filled. The honeycombs grow bigger and bigger.

19

When it is time for a swarm, worker bees build special queen cells at the bottom of the honeycomb. The queen lays eggs in these cells. The workers make a special food out of pollen and chemicals from their bodies. This is royal jelly—a food that only young queen bees eat. Workers feed the royal jelly to the new bees in the queen cells. The rich food makes these bees become queen bees.

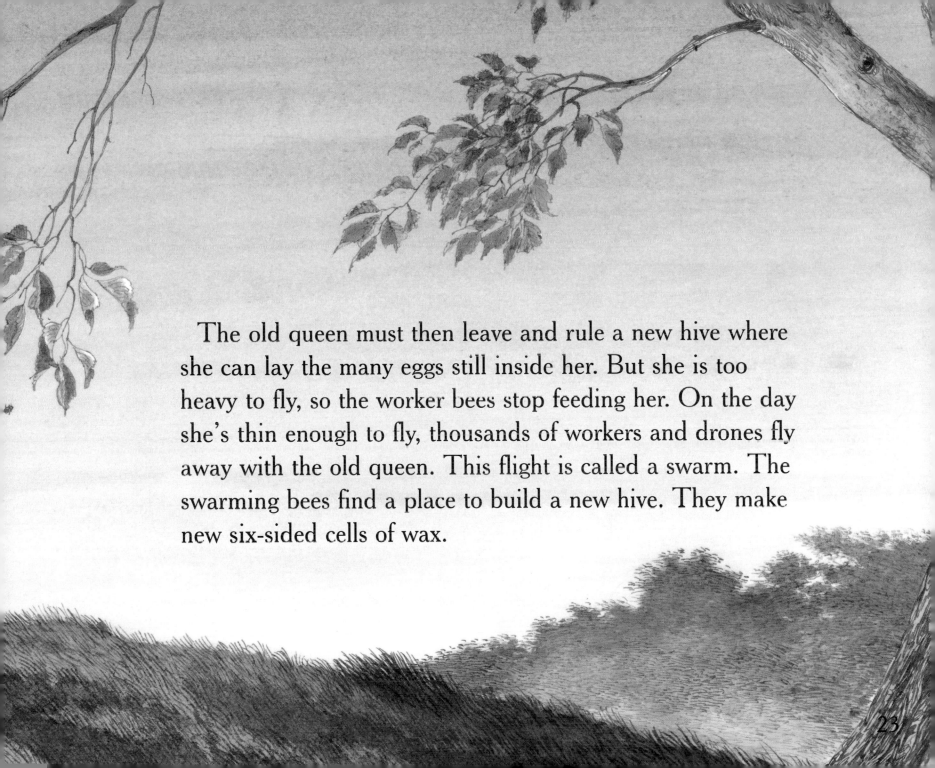

The old queen must then leave and rule a new hive where she can lay the many eggs still inside her. But she is too heavy to fly, so the worker bees stop feeding her. On the day she's thin enough to fly, thousands of workers and drones fly away with the old queen. This flight is called a swarm. The swarming bees find a place to build a new hive. They make new six-sided cells of wax.

Back in the old hive, the new queens fight. The strongest of them kills the others until only she is left. Who will feed her now?

Most of the workers and drones flew off with the old queen. So the new queen must mate right away and lay more eggs. She flies up into the sky for her mating flight, where drones wait for her. She mates in the sky with many drones for about two hours. Then she returns to the hive and lays eggs. Soon new bees fill the hive. New workers search for nectar and bring it back to the hive. More honey is made.

Not only bees love honey. People do, too. Some people gather wild honey, and some build beehives.

For many thousands of years, people all over the world have observed bees and tried to learn all they can about them to get the honey bees make.

Do you love to spread honey on your breakfast toast? Have you ever eaten honey in the honeycomb? Try it sometime. It is delicious combined with its chewy wax. Take a good look at the honeycomb before it's all gone. You will see how well bees build their honeycombs with thin wax.

Look at the label on a jar of honey. It will usually tell you
what kind of flowers the honey came from.

Most of the honey we buy comes from clover, but some comes from wildflowers and some from orange blossoms. Every kind of flower has nectar, and bees gather it wherever they find it.

And every drop of honey tastes just as sweet as a flower smells.

FIND OUT MORE ABOUT BEES AND HONEY

- Bees have a body temperature of 92–93 degrees Fahrenheit in their nest, no matter what the outside temperature is.
- A honeybee would have to fly about 55,000 miles to bring in enough nectar to make one pound of honey.
- It would take a honeybee approximately 1,600 round trips (hive to flower and back to hive again) in order to produce one ounce of honey.
- Honeybees will fly as far as 8 miles from their nest in search of food, at speeds of up to 15 miles per hour.
- The brain of a worker honeybee is about one cubic millimeter, approximately the size of the head of a pin.
- Honeybees' wings stroke 11,400 times per minute and cause a buzzing noise.
- A honeybee would have to visit 2 million flowers to make one pound of honey.
- A honeybee worker visits more than 2,000 flowers on a busy day.
- The average honeybee worker makes $1/12$ teaspoon of honey in her lifetime.
- Honeybees are the only insects that produce food for humans.
- Queen bees will lay as many as 2,000 eggs on a good day, an average of one every 45 seconds.
- Honey has been used for thousands of years as a dressing to help heal wounds.
- In ancient Egypt, people valued honey so highly that it was often used to pay debts.

- In ancient Greece, people offered honey as a tribute to the gods and to spirits of the dead.
- When the first European settlers arrived in North America, they used honey to make cement and furniture polish and to preserve fruits.